A LIFEGUIDE  BIBLE STUDY

# GALATIANS
## Why God Accepts Us

*12 Studies*
*for individuals or groups*

Jack Kuhatschek

With Notes for Leaders

INTERVARSITY PRESS
DOWNERS GROVE, ILLINOIS 60515

InterVarsity Press is the book-publishing division of Inter-Varsity Christian Fellowship, a student movement active on campus at hundreds of universities, colleges and schools of nursing. For information about local and regional activities, write IVCF, 233 Langdon St., Madison, WI 53703.

Cover photograph: Peter French

ISBN 0-8308-1011-0

Printed in the United States of America

| 20 | 19 | 18 | 17 | 16 | 15 | 14 | 13 | 12 | 11 | 10 | 9 | 8 | 7 |
| 99 | 98 | 97 | 96 | 95 | 94 | 93 | 92 | 91 | | | | | |

# Contents

# Getting the Most
# from LifeGuide Bible Studies

Many of us long to fill our minds and our lives with Scripture. We desire to be transformed by its message. LifeGuide Bible Studies are designed to be an exciting and challenging way to do just that. They help us to be guided by God's Word in every area of life.

## How They Work

LifeGuides have a number of distinctive features. Perhaps the most important is that they are *inductive* rather than *deductive*. In other words, they lead us to *discover* what the Bible says rather than simply *telling* us what it says.

They are also thought provoking. They help us to think about the meaning of the passage so that we can truly understand what the author is saying. The questions require more than one-word answers.

The studies are personal. Questions expose us to the promises, assurances, exhortations and challenges of God's Word. They are designed to allow the Scriptures to renew our minds so that we can be transformed by the Spirit of God. This is the ultimate goal of all Bible study.

The studies are versatile. They are designed for student, neighborhood and church groups. They are also effective for individual study.

## How They're Put Together

LifeGuides also have a distinctive format. Each study need take no more than forty-five minutes in a group setting or thirty minutes in personal study—unless you choose to take more time.

The studies can be used within a quarter system in a church and fit well in a semester or trimester system on a college campus. If a guide has more than thirteen studies, it is divided into two or occasionally three parts of approximately twelve studies each.

LifeGuides use a workbook format. Space is provided for writing answers to each question. This is ideal for personal study and allows group members to prepare in advance for the discussion.

The studies also contain leader's notes. They show how to lead a group discussion, provide additional background information on certain questions, give helpful tips on group dynamics and suggest ways to deal with problems which may arise during the discussion. With such helps, someone with little or no experience can lead an effective study.

**Suggestions for Individual Study**

1. As you begin each study, pray that God will help you to understand and apply the passage to your life.

2. Read and reread the assigned Bible passage to familiarize yourself with what the author is saying. In the case of book studies, you may want to read through the entire book prior to the first study. This will give you a helpful overview of its contents.

3. A good modern translation of the Bible, rather than the King James Version or a paraphrase, will give you the most help. The New International Version, the New American Standard Bible and the Revised Standard Version are all recommended. However, the questions in this guide are based on the New International Version.

4. Write your answers in the space provided in the study guide. This will help you to express your understanding of the passage clearly.

5. It might be good to have a Bible dictionary handy. Use it to look up any unfamiliar words, names or places.

**Suggestions for Group Study**

1. Come to the study prepared. Follow the suggestions for individual study mentioned above. You will find that careful preparation will greatly enrich your time spent in group discussion.

2. Be willing to participate in the discussion. The leader of your group will not be lecturing. Instead, he or she will be encouraging the members of the group to discuss what they have learned from the passage. The leader will be asking the questions that are found in this guide. Plan to share what God has taught you in your individual study.

3. Stick to the passage being studied. Your answers should be based on the verses which are the focus of the discussion and not on outside authorities such as commentaries or speakers. This guide deliberately avoids jumping

from book to book or passage to passage. Each study focuses on only one passage. Book studies are generally designed to lead you through the book in the order in which it was written. This will help you follow the author's argument.

4. Be sensitive to the other members of the group. Listen attentively when they share what they have learned. You may be surprised by their insights! Link what you say to the comments of others so the group stays on the topic. Also, be affirming whenever you can. This will encourage some of the more hesitant members of the group to participate.

5. Be careful not to dominate the discussion. We are sometimes so eager to share what we have learned that we leave too little opportunity for others to respond. By all means participate! But allow others to also.

6. Expect God to teach you through the passage being discussed and through the other members of the group. Pray that you will have an enjoyable and profitable time together.

7. If you are the discussion leader, you will find additional suggestions and helpful ideas for each study in the leader's notes. These are found at the back of the guide.

# Introducing Galatians

We all want to be accepted—by our family, by our friends and most of all by God. But so often people accept us only *if* we are attractive, smart, wealthy or powerful. So we work hard to project the right image and to conceal our faults.

We often transfer this attitude to our relationship with God. We feel we must earn his acceptance. If we could only work harder, live better, pray longer, witness to more people—then we might get on God's good side.

In Galatians Paul challenges this kind of thinking. He exposes the futility of trying to earn God's acceptance when we are already accepted in Christ. His message frees us from living out of a sense of guilt. We find fresh assurance of God's love and renewed power to serve him.

Galatians was written by Paul sometime between A.D. 48-49. It was probably addressed to the churches in Antioch, Iconium, Lystra and Derbe, which were located in the Roman province of Galatia. Paul and Barnabas visited these cities during their first missionary journey. Their reception was unforgettable. Acts 13—14 tells us that they were driven out of Antioch, that they fled from Iconium and that Paul was stoned in Lystra! Yet in spite of the opposition against Paul and Barnabas, people believed the gospel and churches were formed.

The real threat arose shortly thereafter. Certain people infiltrated the new churches with a different message. "Paul omitted an important part of the gospel," they claimed. "You must also be circumcised and keep the law of Moses if you want to be saved" (see Acts 15:1). Their arguments were impressive and their religious zeal was undeniable. The Galatians were almost persuaded when Paul received word of what was happening. Quickly he dictated this letter and sent it to be read in each of the churches. Centuries later it still radiates the heat of Paul's anger. These preachers were impostors.

Their gospel was perverted. The Galatians were in grave danger!

This study guide introduces you to the most passionate and forceful letter in the New Testament. It consists of twelve forty-five minute studies. The first eleven allow you to interact with and apply the main idea in each passage. In the final study you review the letter. You also grapple with some contemporary issues which are related to those problems faced by Paul and the Galatians.

# 1
# Good News and Bad
## *Galatians 1:1-10*

The church has always been plagued by false teachers, heretics and followers of various cults. Usually such people have an aggressive program for winning new converts. How are we to respond to those who preach or accept a twisted gospel? Paul gives us an example in this passage.

The letter to the Galatians begins abruptly. After the salutation in verses 1-5, Paul omits the customary expression of thanksgiving we find in his letters to the Ephesians, Philippians, Colossians and others. Instead, he plunges immediately into an impassioned discussion of some astonishing news he has heard about the Galatians.

**1.** If a close Christian friend of yours was almost persuaded to join a cult, how would you respond?

**2.** Read Galatians 1:1-10. How would you describe the mood of this passage?

**3.** The word *apostle* means "one who is sent." According to verse 1, who sent Paul and who did not?

Why would he be concerned about this distinction?

**4.** In three brief verses (3-5), Paul tells us an enormous amount about the gospel. What do we learn?

Which aspect of the gospel do you especially need now? Explain.

**5.** In verses 6-7 Paul summarizes the problem which caused him to write this letter. What was happening in the Galatian churches?

Why was it so astonishing to Paul?

**6.** Verse 6 implies that if we desert the gospel we also desert God. Why would this be true?

**7.** Why do you think Paul is so harsh in his judgment of those who preach a different gospel (vv. 8-9)?

**8.** How might the way we present the gospel be different if we were seeking the approval of people instead of God (v. 10)?

**9.** What are some ways the gospel is being perverted today?

**10.** According to this passage, how can we ensure that the gospel we believe and preach is the true gospel?

# 2
# Why Believe the Gospel?
## *Galatians 1:11—2:10*

Have you ever been talking with someone about the gospel when suddenly he or she says, "But that's just *your* opinion!"? This raises an important question. If the gospel is merely our opinion, then why should they listen to us? There are many other religions in the world, each one claiming to be a path to God. Who are we to assert that the gospel is the only true message of salvation?

This objection isn't new. Paul's opponents questioned the authenticity of the gospel he preached. In this passage he sets out to describe and defend the source of his gospel. In so doing he tells us why the gospel message is unique.

---

**1.** What is the primary reason why you believe the gospel is true and not just a nice story?

---

**2.** Read Galatians 1:11—2:10. In 1:11-12 Paul claims he received the gospel from Jesus Christ, not men. How does his brief autobiography in 1:13-24 confirm this claim?

**3.** What practical difference would it make to the Galatians whether Paul received his gospel from men or from God?

**4.** What practical difference does it make to you?

**5.** Paul obviously did not need human authorization to preach the gospel. Why then did he present his gospel to the leaders in Jerusalem (2:1-2)?

**6.** Why was it significant that Titus (a Gentile) was not compelled to be circumcised (the sign of becoming a Jew)?

**7.** Paul refused to give in to false brothers on the matter of circumcision "so that the truth of the gospel might remain with you" (2:5). How do you show your concern to preserve the gospel?

**8.** How did the leaders in Jerusalem respond to Paul's message and ministry (2:6-10)?

Why was their endorsement of Paul's gospel and ministry important both then and now?

**9.** The apostles were not simply zealous to preserve the gospel. They also felt called to proclaim the gospel (2:7-10). To whom do you feel called to go with the gospel?

**10.** What step can you take this week to bring the good news to someone?

**11.** How can Paul's testimony in this passage increase our confidence in the truth of the gospel?

# 3
# Accepting Others

## *Galatians 2:11-21*

Have you ever felt like avoiding certain types of Christians? Perhaps you don't like their theology. You may disapprove of their lifestyle. Or you may prefer to avoid people of their race, nationality or economic background. This passage helps us see why such attitudes conflict with the basic message of the gospel.

**1.** What types or groups of Christians do you feel like avoiding? Why?

**2.** Read Galatians 2:11-21. How were Peter and the other Jews not "acting in line with the truth of the gospel" (vv. 11-14)?

**3.** How might their actions have forced "Gentiles to follow Jewish customs" (v. 14)?

**4.** What nonessential customs do Christians sometimes force on each other?

**5.** Why is it wrong to make such customs a basis for fellowship (vv. 15-16)?

**6.** *To justify* (vv. 15-17) is a legal term meaning the person on trial is declared not guilty and deserves all the privileges of one who has not broken the law. How might justification by faith lead some to claim that "Christ promotes sin" (v. 17)?

**7.** How does Paul refute this accusation (vv. 17-19)?

**8.** How has Christ enabled us to die to the law and to live for God (v. 20)?

**9.** Practically speaking, what does it mean to live for God?

**10.** If we have died to the law as a means of being accepted by God, how should this affect our self-image?

**11.** How should God's acceptance of us affect our attitude toward other Christians—even those from different races, backgrounds and traditions?

# 4
# Why God Accepts Us
## *Galatians 3:1-14*

We all want to be accepted. We do everything we can to win people's approval and avoid their rejection. But if we work so hard to please people, then what about God? How can we possibly meet his standards?

The Galatians felt these inner struggles. They wanted to be fully accepted by God. But they seemed to forget that God had already accepted them. They also forgot *why.* In fact, their thinking became so mixed up that Paul wondered if they had been bewitched! In 3:1-14 he sets out to break the "spell" they are under by asking five pointed questions and examining six key Old Testament passages.

---

**1.** Do you ever feel unacceptable to God? Explain.

---

**2.** Read Galatians 3:1-14. From verses 1-5 try to reconstruct in chronological order the Galatians' spiritual biography.

**3.** In what ways did the Galatians' behavior seem "bewitched" and "foolish" according to verses 1-5?

**4.** In what ways do we sometimes try to earn God's favor by what we do?

**5.** How can a vivid image of Christ's crucifixion (v. 1) guard us from this warped way of thinking?

**6.** When we follow the example of Abraham's faith, what are the results (vv. 6-9)?

**7.** How does Abraham's experience contrast with that of the person who seeks to earn God's acceptance (vv. 10-12)?

**8.** The word *redeemed* means to deliver from some evil by paying a price. How and why did Christ redeem us (vv. 13-14)?

**9.** How have you been blessed by the Spirit's presence in your life (v. 14)?

**10.** How does the gift of the Spirit affirm that God accepts us completely in Christ?

**11.** There are several key words in verses 1-14 which describe what Christ has done for us. Identify some of these, then spend time thanking God for each one.

# 5
# Exposing Our Needs
## *Galatians 3:15-29*

Honey," Jill called out, "you'd better call the repairman. Our TV is on the blink again."

"Who needs a repairman!" Ron replied confidently. "I can fix this myself."

Four hours later. "There, that should do it." As he plugs it in, there's a loud buzzing noise, smoke rises from the TV, the lights begin to flicker, then darkness blacks out the room.

"Uh . . . maybe you're right, dear," Ron said sheepishly. "I suppose calling a repairman couldn't hurt."

People must admit they need help before they can receive it. Yet often this is very difficult. In Galatians 3:15-29 Paul tells us how God exposes our need for Christ.

**1.** Why is admitting we have a problem often so difficult for us?

**2.** Read Galatians 3:15-29. Why is the law unable to set aside or add to the promises spoken to Abraham (vv. 15-18)?

**3.** If the law did not set aside or add to the promises given to Abraham, then why was it given (vv. 19-25)?

**4.** When you were a non-Christian, to what extent did you realize that you were a prisoner of sin (v. 22)?

**5.** How might a clear grasp of God's law have helped you to realize your need of Christ (vv. 22-25)?

**6.** How then should a knowledge of the law's purpose affect our evangelism?

**7.** In verse 28 Paul lists several ways in which people have been categorized. How have these categories sometimes functioned as barriers?

**8.** In light of the context, how have these barriers been broken down in Christ?

**9.** In what practical ways should this affect our relationships with the groups mentioned in verse 28?

**10.** Jesus once told a Pharisee that a person who is forgiven little loves little, but a person who is forgiven much loves much (Lk 7:36-50). How has a knowledge of your former condition increased your love and appreciation of Christ?

# 6
# The Joys of Growing Up
## *Galatians 4:1-20*

Have you ever longed to be a child again—to be free from work, mortgage payments, bills and taxes? Remember the carefree days, when from morning till night your job was to play? The Galatians did. They longed to return to the spiritual childhood of the law. But aren't we forgetting something? Just think of all the things we *couldn't* do as children. In Galatians 4:1-20 Paul reminds us of the joys of growing up.

**1.** In what ways do adults have greater privileges than children?

**2.** Read Galatians 4:1-20. In verses 1-2 Paul refers to practices in Roman society. How was a Roman child no different from a slave?

**3.** How was life under the law like spiritual childhood (vv. 3-7)?

**4.** Verse 4 states, "When the time had fully come, God sent his Son." How did things change because of his coming (vv. 4-7)?

**5.** God has also sent the Spirit of his Son into our hearts, calling out, "*Abba,* Father" (v. 6). In what ways have you experienced an intimate relationship with the Father?

**6.** In view of Paul's discussion in verses 1-7, how does the Galatians' behavior seem incredible (vv. 8-11)?

**7.** In what ways do you sometimes act like a spiritual slave?

How can you begin acting more like God's beloved son or daughter?

**8.** How and why had the Galatians' attitude toward Paul changed (vv. 12-20)?

**9.** What do these verses reveal about Paul's feelings toward the Galatians?

_____

**10.** How do verses 12-20 illustrate the care and concern we should have for other members of God's family?

_____

**11.** Spend a few minutes of intimate prayer with the Father, thanking him for the privileges of being a member of his family.

# 7
# Do-It-Yourself Religion
## *Galatians 4:21—5:1*

T rusting God can seem risky. What if he lets us down? Still worse, what if our faith is simply foolishness? When such thoughts enter our minds, it's easy to panic. We are tempted to take back what we have entrusted to God. We feel safer taking matters into our own hands.

Abraham felt these struggles while waiting for God's promise of a son. He rushed God's plan and had a son through his slave Hagar. Later, even though he and Sarah were very old, the promised son was born. This story has become a timeless illustration of do-it-yourself religion versus trust in the promises of God.

This study will consider Paul's unusual treatment of the story of Hagar and Sarah. Brace yourself! We will be introduced to women who are compared to covenants, mountains and even cities.

---

**1.** Why are we often uncomfortable in situations where we aren't in control (for example, a roller coaster, a sickness and so on)?

---

**2.** Read Galatians 4:21—5:1. How were Abraham's two sons (Ishmael and Isaac) different according to verses 21-23?

**3.** What does Paul mean when he says that the son of the slave woman was born the "ordinary way," but the son of the free woman was "the result of a promise" (v. 23; see also v. 29)?

**4.** In verse 24 Paul says that the story of Hagar and Sarah may be understood "figuratively" (NIV) or "allegorically" (NASB). What do Hagar, the covenant from Sinai and "the present city of Jerusalem" have in common (vv. 24-25)?

**5.** How is Sarah (who, although unnamed, is the other woman in the story) similar to the new covenant and to the Jerusalem that is above (vv. 26-27)?

**6.** How do the two sons, two covenants and two cities illustrate two radically different views we can have about salvation?

**7.** Paul states that just as Ishmael persecuted Isaac, so too those born the ordinary way still persecute those born by the power of the Spirit (v. 29). How have you seen this to be true, even in your own life?

**8.** How does Paul describe the ultimate fate of the slave woman's and the free woman's spiritual descendants (v. 30)?

**9.** The spiritual principle described in this passage has broad application. Throughout Scripture God promises to accomplish that which we cannot do on our own. Think of Abraham, Moses, Joshua, Gideon, the apostles and others. In what areas are you trusting in the promises of God and the power of the Spirit to accomplish the extraordinary?

**10.** In 5:1 Paul states that Christ set us free so that we could experience freedom! Given the thrust of Galatians 1—4, what does Paul mean when he says we are free?

**11.** What are some present-day threats to our spiritual freedom?

What are some practical ways we can "stand firm" against them?

# 8
# A Severe Warning

## *Galatians 5:2-12*

H elp!" the man cried as he dangled helplessly from the edge of a cliff. "Can anyone up there help me?"

"Yes," answered a heavenly voice, "I'll help you. But first you must let go."

"Let go!" gasped the man. "But then I'd fall!"

"I'll catch you," replied the voice.

There was a long pause, then the man cried out, "Can anyone *else* up there help me?"

If we want Christ to save us, we must let go of the idea that we can save ourselves—even a little. Up to this point Paul has passionately argued for justification by faith in Christ. He has also ruthlessly demonstrated the futility of seeking righteousness by the law. Now the Galatians must decide between law or grace—they *cannot* have both. This is perhaps the most severe warning in all of Paul's writings.

**1.** Proverbs 27:6 states: "Wounds from a friend are better than kisses from an enemy!" (LB). Why do you think this is true?

**2.** Read Galatians 5:2-12. What were the Judaizers (those preaching against Paul) urging the Galatians to do and why (vv. 2-4)?

**3.** In your own words explain the consequences of trying to be justified by law (vv. 2-4).

**4.** Paul's warning probably surprised the Galatians. They knew faith in Christ was *necessary* for their salvation; they simply wondered whether it was *sufficient*. Why does any attempt to earn God's acceptance destroy justification by faith?

**5.** In verses 2-4 Paul gave stern warnings to those who desired to be circumcised. Now he says "neither circumcision nor uncircumcision has any value" (v. 6). How can both of these views be true?

**6.** In verse 6 we might have expected Paul to say, "The only thing that counts is faith." How does his actual statement give us a balanced view of the Christian life?

**7.** Give examples of how we can express our faith through loving acts.

**8.** Paul compares the Galatians to runners in a race and to a batch of dough (vv. 7-9). How do these comparisons illustrate the nature and perils of the Christian life?

**9.** Considering the seriousness of the threat facing the Galatians, how would you explain Paul's confident statement in the first half of verse 10?

**10.** In verses 10-12 Paul makes some severe statements about those who are troubling the Galatians (especially v. 12!). Even by today's standards they are harsh. Why was he so upset?

**11.** In Paul's day the cross was offensive (v. 11) because it declared that circumcision and law-keeping were unnecessary for justification. Why is the cross offensive today?

**12.** What must happen in people's minds and hearts before they can become thankful for the cross?

How can we help in this process?

# 9
# Living by the Spirit
## *Galatians 5:13-26*

If Christ has set us free, then why not live as we please? Why not grab all the money, sex and power we can get? Afterward, we can simply ask for forgiveness!

Paul challenges this kind of thinking in Galatians 5. First, he explains the true meaning of Christian freedom. Then he describes how our lives can be transformed by the Spirit.

---

**1.** Imagine that all civil and criminal laws were abolished in your community. How and why might this affect the people who live there?

---

**2.** Read Galatians 5:13-26. What is the difference between the two concepts of freedom described in verses 13-14?

---

**3.** In verse 15 Paul accuses the Galatians of "biting and devouring each other." Where do you see these practices among Christians today?

How would Paul's exhortations in verses 13-14 provide a remedy to this type of conduct?

**4.** What does it mean to "live by the Spirit" (v. 16)?

**5.** If we live by the Spirit, what does Paul assure us will happen (vv. 16-17)?

**6.** How is being led by the Spirit different than living under law (v. 18)?

**7.** Why is it so easy to recognize the acts of the sinful nature (vv. 19-21)?

**8.** How can Paul's warning in verse 21 be reconciled with his emphasis on justification by faith?

**9.** Why is *fruit* a good description of the Spirit's work in us (vv. 22-23)?

**10.** In what ways do you see the Spirit's fruit ripening in your life?

**11.** Paul assumes that even though all Christians live by the Spirit, we do not always keep in step with the Spirit (vv. 25-26). In what ways do you struggle to keep in step with the Spirit?

**12.** Spend time thanking God for the Spirit's work in your life. Pray for the Spirit's help in those areas where you feel out of step.

# 10
# The Law of Love

## *Galatians 6:1-10*

The fruit of the Spirit is most clearly demonstrated in our relationships with others. They are a visible and practical measure of our spirituality. In this passage Paul describes how we should relate to the family of believers and to all people.

---

**1.** Read Galatians 6:1-10 and identify the various relationships Paul has in view.

---

**2.** Describe how you might feel if you were "caught in a sin" (v. 1).

What guidelines does Paul offer for dealing with such a person, and why is each important?

**3.** What types of burdens might Paul have had in mind in verse 2?

What are some ways you might help a fellow Christian to carry these?

**4.** How does the law of Christ (v. 2) differ from the kind of law-keeping urged by Paul's opponents?

**5.** The sins or burdens of others can lead us to feel superior. How can proper methods of self-examination correct this attitude (vv. 3-5)?

**6.** The idea of a Christian teacher receiving remuneration (v. 6) might seem unspiritual to some. What are some practical reasons Paul may have commanded this?

**7.** Paul describes the principle of sowing and reaping in verses 7-8. One person has expanded these verses as follows:
Sow a thought, reap an act.
Sow an act, reap a habit.
Sow a habit, reap a character.
Sow a character, reap a destiny.

Do you think this is an accurate and helpful understanding of these verses? Explain why or why not.

**8.** What other application of the principle of sowing and reaping does Paul make in verses 9 and 10?

**9.** What are one or two new ways you could begin sowing to please the Spirit (a) personally, (b) in relationships with other Christians and (c) in relationships with non-Christians?

# 11
# Getting Motivated
## *Galatians 6:11-18*

Peer pressure can exert a powerful influence on us. The style of our clothes, the kind of music we listen to, our vocabulary, even the soft drinks we buy are affected by what others do and say. We are often tempted to change our behavior so others will accept us. But such approval can have a high price tag. In this final passage Paul helps us to consider whose approval we desire most.

Paul normally dictated his letters while another wrote them down. At this point, however, he asks for the pen and writes the final words of this book in large letters—probably for emphasis. Here we look into the heart of both Paul and his opponents. We find their motives are as different as their messages.

**1.** Why do you think people are so concerned about being accepted by their peers?

**2.** Read Galatians 6:11-18. What do verses 12-13 reveal about the motives of Paul's opponents?

**3.** How would urging others to be circumcised help them to achieve their goals?

**4.** The approval of others was most important to Paul's opponents (v. 12). In what situations are you tempted to hide your Christianity in order to "make a good impression outwardly"?

**5.** F. F. Bruce writes, "It is difficult, after sixteen centuries and more during which the cross has been a sacred symbol, to realize the unspeakable horror and loathing which the very mention or thought of the cross provoked in Paul's day."[1] Yet in spite of this the cross was Paul's ground for boasting (v. 14)! What does it mean to boast in the cross?

How does it differ from the boasting of Paul's opponents?

**6.** How will boasting in the cross affect our desire for the world's approval (v. 14)?

How will it affect the world's attitude toward us?

---

**7.** Why does the new creation have value in contrast to the worthlessness of circumcision or uncircumcision (v. 15)?

---

**8.** In Paul's closing blessing and benediction he mentions peace, mercy and the grace of our Lord Jesus Christ (vv. 16, 18). Why is each of these appropriate for those who follow the "rule" of verses 14-15?

---

**9.** Two of the false accusations against Paul were that he tried to please men rather than God (1:10), and that he still preached circumcision (5:11). How does verse 17 provide a powerful refutation of these claims?

**10.** Paul bore on his body the marks of Jesus (the evidence of faithful service). What are the "marks of Jesus" in your life?

---

**11.** How has this passage helped to purify your motives and goals in life?

---

[1] F. F. Bruce, *The Epistle to the Galatians,* The New International Greek Commentary (Grand Rapids, Mich.: Eerdmans, 1982), p. 271.

# 12
# Galatians Today

## *Galatians 1—6*

T he book of Galatians was written to counteract some specific problems faced by Christians in the first century. Today we no longer encounter these exact same problems. After all, when was the last time someone urged you to be circumcised as a means of salvation? Yet we would be mistaken to think the problems no longer exist. They do exist—but their appearance has changed, making them difficult to recognize.

This study involves more than a review of Galatians. You will also grapple with how the principles you've learned in Galatians apply to problems we face today.

**1.** As you think back over the book of Galatians, what major themes come to mind? Briefly summarize Paul's position on each one.

**2.** Throughout this letter Paul has referred to "the gospel." From what he has said, what are the most important elements of the gospel?

**3.** What things must be excluded from any presentation of the gospel or any proper response to the gospel?

**4.** It is not uncommon for people to try to pit the teachings of Jesus against those of Paul. For example, one person has written: "Luther and Calvin, we know, looked to the book of Romans in the Bible for their primary inspiration. Were they, unknowingly, possessed more by the Spirit of St. Paul than by the Spirit of Jesus Christ? Are we not on safer grounds if we look to our Lord's words to launch our reformation?" How would Paul have responded to this statement?

**5.** Critique the following in light of what you have learned in Galatians: "What must I do to be justified? Three things:
a. I must believe in Jesus Christ and thereby receive the forgiveness he offers through his death on the cross.
b. I must be baptized.
c. I must seek to obey the commandments of God with the help of his Spirit. If I faithfully do all of these, then God will accept me into his eternal kingdom." Is this a true or perverted statement of the gospel? Explain your answer.

**6.** Can someone be saved who firmly believes in a false or perverted gospel? Defend your position from what Paul has said in this letter.

---

**7.** Today many churches and Christian schools legislate rules for their members or students. These rules often oppose such practices as drinking alcoholic beverages, smoking, dancing, going to movies and so on. Those who make and enforce these rules are often criticized and labeled as "legalistic." Do you think this criticism is valid or invalid? Why?

---

**8.** What have you appreciated most about your study of Galatians?

# Leader's Notes

Leading a Bible discussion can be an enjoyable and rewarding experience. But it can also be *scary*—especially if you've never done it before. If this is your feeling, you're in good company. When God asked Moses to lead the Israelites out of Egypt, he replied, "O Lord, please send someone else to do it!" (Ex 4:13).

When Solomon became king of Israel, he felt the task was far beyond his abilities. "I am only a little child and do not know how to carry out my duties. . . . Who is able to govern this great people of yours?" (1 Kings 3:7, 9).

When God called Jeremiah to be a prophet, he replied, "Ah, Sovereign LORD, . . . I do not know how to speak; I am only a child" (Jer 1:6).

The list goes on. The apostles were "unschooled, ordinary men" (Acts 4:13). Timothy was young, frail and frightened. Paul's "thorn in the flesh" made him feel weak. But God's response to all of his servants—including you—is essentially the same: "My grace is sufficient for you" (2 Cor 12:9). Relax. God helped these people in spite of their weaknesses, and he can help you in spite of your feelings of inadequacy.

There is another reason why you should feel encouraged. Leading a Bible discussion is not difficult if you follow certain guidelines. You don't need to be an expert on the Bible or a trained teacher. The suggestions listed below should enable you to effectively and enjoyably fulfill your role as leader.

## Preparing to Lead

1. Ask God to help you understand and apply the passage to your own life. Unless this happens, you will not be prepared to lead others. Pray too for the various members of the group. Ask God to give you an enjoyable and profitable time together studying his Word.

**2.** As you begin each study, read and reread the assigned Bible passage to familiarize yourself with what the author is saying. In the case of book studies, you may want to read through the entire book prior to the first study. This will give you a helpful overview of its contents.

**3.** This study guide is based on the New International Version of the Bible. It will help you and the group if you use this translation as the basis for your study and discussion. Encourage others to use the NIV also, but allow them the freedom to use whatever translation they prefer.

**4.** Carefully work through each question in the study. Spend time in meditation and reflection as you formulate your answers.

**5.** Write your answers in the space provided in the study guide. This will help you to express your understanding of the passage clearly.

**6.** It might help you to have a Bible dictionary handy. Use it to look up any unfamiliar words, names or places. (For additional help on how to study a passage, see chapter five of *Leading Bible Discussions,* IVP.)

**7.** Once you have finished your own study of the passage, familiarize yourself with the leader's notes for the study you are leading. These are designed to help you in several ways. First, they tell you the purpose the study guide author had in mind while writing the study. Take time to think through how the study questions work together to accomplish that purpose. Second, the notes provide you with additional background information or comments on some of the questions. This information can be useful if people have difficulty understanding or answering a question. Third, the leader's notes can alert you to potential problems you may encounter during the study.

**8.** If you wish to remind yourself of anything mentioned in the leader's notes, make a note to yourself below that question in the study.

## Leading the Study

**1.** Begin the study on time. Unless you are leading an evangelistic Bible study, open with prayer, asking God to help you to understand and apply the passage.

**2.** Be sure that everyone in your group has a study guide. Encourage them to prepare beforehand for each discussion by working through the questions in the guide.

**3.** At the beginning of your first time together, explain that these studies are meant to be discussions not lectures. Encourage the members of the group to participate. However, do not put pressure on those who may be hesitant to speak during the first few sessions.

**4.** Read the introductory paragraph at the beginning of the discussion. This will orient the group to the passage being studied.

**5.** Read the passage aloud if you are studying one chapter or less. You may choose to do this yourself, or someone else may read if he or she has been asked to do so prior to the study. Longer passages may occasionally be read in parts at different times during the study. Some studies may cover several chapters. In such cases reading aloud would probably take too much time, so the group members should simply read the assigned passages prior to the study.

**6.** As you begin to ask the questions in the guide, keep several things in mind. First, the questions are designed to be used just as they are written. If you wish, you may simply read them aloud to the group. Or you may prefer to express them in your own words. However, unnecessary rewording of the questions is not recommended.

Second, the questions are intended to guide the group toward understanding and applying the *main idea* of the passage. The author of the guide has stated his or her view of this central idea in the *purpose* of the study in the leader's notes. You should try to understand how the passage expresses this idea and how the study questions work together to lead the group in that direction.

There may be times when it is appropriate to deviate from the study guide. For example, a question may have already been answered. If so, move on to the next question. Or someone may raise an important question not covered in the guide. Take time to discuss it! The important thing is to use discretion. There may be many routes you can travel to reach the goal of the study. But the easiest route is usually the one the author has suggested.

**7.** Avoid answering your own questions. If necessary, repeat or rephrase them until they are clearly understood. An eager group quickly becomes passive and silent if they think the leader will do most of the talking.

**8.** Don't be afraid of silence. People may need time to think about the question before formulating their answers.

**9.** Don't be content with just one answer. Ask, "What do the rest of you think?" or "Anything else?" until several people have given answers to the question.

**10.** Acknowledge all contributions. Try to be affirming whenever possible. Never reject an answer. If it is clearly wrong, ask, "Which verse led you to that conclusion?" or again, "What do the rest of you think?"

**11.** Don't expect every answer to be addressed to you, even though this will probably happen at first. As group members become more at ease, they will begin to truly interact with each other. This is one sign of a healthy discussion.

**12.** Don't be afraid of controversy. It can be very stimulating. If you don't resolve an issue completely, don't be frustrated. Move on and keep it in mind for later. A subsequent study may solve the problem.

**13.** Stick to the passage under consideration. It should be the source for answering the questions. Discourage the group from unnecessary cross-referencing. Likewise, stick to the subject and avoid going off on tangents.

**14.** Periodically summarize what the *group* has said about the passage. This helps to draw together the various ideas mentioned and gives continuity to the study. But don't preach.

**15.** Conclude your time together with conversational prayer. Be sure to ask God's help to apply those things which you learned in the study.

**16.** End on time.

Many more suggestions and helps are found in *Leading Bible Discussions* (IVP). Reading and studying through that would be well worth your time.

## Components of Small Groups

A healthy small group should do more than study the Bible. There are four components you should consider as you structure your time together.

*Nurture.* Being a part of a small group should be a nurturing and edifying experience. You should grow in your knowledge and love of God and each other. If we are to properly love God, we must know and keep his commandments (Jn 14:15). That is why Bible study should be a foundational part of your small group. But you can be nurtured by other things as well. You can memorize Scripture, read and discuss a book, or occasionally listen to a tape of a good speaker.

*Community.* Most people have a need for close friendships. Your small group can be an excellent place to cultivate such relationships. Allow time for informal interaction before and after the study. Have a time of sharing during the meeting. Do fun things together as a group, such as a potluck supper or a picnic. Have someone bring refreshments to the meeting. Be creative!

*Worship.* A portion of your time together can be spent in worship and prayer. Praise God together for who he is. Thank him for what he has done and is doing in your lives and in the world. Pray for each other's needs. Ask God to help you to apply what you have learned. Sing hymns together.

*Mission.* Many small groups decide to work together in some form of outreach. This can be a practical way of applying what you have learned. You can host a series of evangelistic discussions for your friends or neighbors. You can visit people at a home for the elderly. Help a widow with cleaning or repair jobs around her home. Such projects can have a transforming influence on your group.

For a detailed discussion of the nature and function of small groups, read *Small Group Leaders' Handbook* or *Good Things Come in Small Groups* (both from IVP).

**Study 1. Good News and Bad. Galatians 1:1-10.**

*Purpose:* To understand the importance of believing and preaching the true gospel and the dangers associated with embracing a perverted gospel.

You may wish to begin the study by reading aloud the introduction on pages 8-9 or by summarizing its content. If everyone has read it prior to the study, you can briefly go over the main points.

**Question 1.** Almost every study begins with an "approach" question, which is meant to be asked *before* the passage is read. These questions are important for several reasons.

First, they help the group to warm up to each other. No matter how well a group may know each other or how comfortable they may be with each other, there is always a stiffness that needs to be overcome before people will begin to talk openly. A good question will break the ice.

Second, approach questions get people thinking along the lines of the topic of the study. Most people will have lots of different things going on in their minds (dinner, an important meeting coming up, how to get the car fixed) that will have nothing to do with the study. A creative question will get their attention and draw them into the discussion.

Third, approach questions can reveal where our thoughts or feelings need to be transformed by Scripture. This is why it is especially important *not* to read the passage before the approach question is asked. The passage will tend to color the honest reactions people would otherwise give because they are of course *supposed* to think the way the Bible does. Giving honest responses to various issues before they find out what the Bible says may help them to see where their thoughts or attitudes need to be changed.

**Question 3.** Someone may wonder what the difference is between "from men" and "by man." "From men" would mean that Paul's commission was from men *only* and not from God. "By man" suggests that God appointed Paul through the agency of man.

Let the group wrestle with this question. Don't be too quick to supply the answer yourself, since this tends to inhibit the discussion.

**Questions 6-7.** If discussion gets stuck on what the gospel is, remind the group of their answers to question 4 concerning verses 3-5.

If someone asks about what Paul meant about being "eternally condemned" (vv. 8-9), you might be helped by John Stott, who writes: "The Greek word twice translated 'eternally condemned' is *anathema*. It was used in the Greek Old Testament for the divine ban, the curse of God resting upon anything or anyone devoted by Him to destruction. The story of Achan provides an example of this. . . . So the apostle Paul desires that these false teachers should come under the divine ban, curse or *anathema*. That is, he expresses the wish that God's judgment will fall on them" (Stott, *The Message of Galatians* [Downers Grove, Ill.: InterVarsity Press, 1968], p. 24).

**Question 8.** Some may have questioned whether Paul changed his message to suit the audience in order to get the widest following wherever he went.

**Question 9.** It may not be wise at this point to expect detailed explanations of how the gospel is being perverted today. The issues involved should become clearer to members of your group as they study further in Galatians.

**Study 2. Why Believe the Gospel? Galatians 1:11—2:10.**
*Purpose:* To realize that the gospel Paul preached came from God not men.

**Question 2.** Each incident Paul relates is intended in some way to prove that his gospel did not come from men but God. There are many other interesting facts about Paul's life in these verses, but be careful not to get sidetracked from the main points.

The visit to Jerusalem mentioned in 1:18-19 is probably the one described in Acts 9:26-30.

**Question 5.** It seems likely that the visit to Jerusalem mentioned in 2:1-10 is the one recorded in Acts 11:29-30 (see also Acts 12:25). But no details are given in Acts about the events described in Galatians 2:1-10.

The revelation mentioned in 2:2 may have been the prophecy of Agabus recorded in Acts 11:27-28. However, the context of Galatians 2:1-10 suggests that God desired a meeting between Paul and the leaders in Jerusalem. Paul's gospel may have been independent of such men, but their endorsement would help to maintain the unity of the church and the continued purity of the gospel.

Paul's statement "for fear that I was running or had run my race in vain" probably didn't mean that he feared he had been preaching the wrong message. This would contradict everything he has said before. Without this meeting in Jerusalem, there are other ways in which Paul's ministry might have been in jeopardy. Urge your group to explore some of these other possibilities.

**Question 6.** Verses 3-5 give some specific statements about some of the issues that were at stake. Focus on these. If the discussion moves too far beyond these verses, remind people that the rest of the letter answers this question more fully.

**Question 7.** Martin Luther wrote, "We will suffer our goods to be taken away, our name, our life, and all we have; but the Gospel, our faith, Jesus Christ, we will never suffer to be wrested from us" ( *Commentary on the Epistle to the Galatians* [Cambridge, England: James Clarke, 1953], p. 108).

### Study 3. Accepting Others. Galatians 2:11-21.

*Purpose:* To realize that we must unconditionally accept other Christians because God has accepted us.

**Questions 2-3.** During the first century, Jews normally did not associate with Gentiles. However, Gentiles could become converts to Judaism by being circumcised and agreeing to obey the law (Ex 12:48-49; Num 15:14-16). Then it would be acceptable to have fellowship with them. The early church wrestled with the question of whether a gentile Christian must also become a Jew in order to be saved. The book of Galatians resulted from that controversy.

**Question 4.** For example, certain ways of praying, certain dress at worship, certain lifestyle habits and so on.

**Question 5.** The incident with Peter becomes a springboard for a broader discussion of justification by faith (vv. 15-21). If God has accepted us unconditionally through Christ, then we must accept other Christians.

**Question 6.** If people have difficulty with this question, then ask, "If salvation isn't based on what *we* do but rather on what *Jesus* has done, then what's to prevent us from sinning? After all, we can always ask for forgiveness later." This issue will be covered more fully in study nine.

**Questions 7-8.** The group may have difficulty understanding verses 18-19. In verse 18 *what I destroyed* probably refers to Paul's trust in the law for justification. Paul knew he couldn't keep the law, so trying to "rebuild" his confidence in the law would be futile.

Don't allow the group to get bogged down on question 7. The main points to notice are that Paul emphatically denies that Christ promotes sin ("absolutely not" v. 17) and that Paul died to the law not in order to sin but rather "so that I might live for God" (v. 19).

In question 8 help the group to see that the demands of the law were fully satisfied when Christ was crucified. When Christ died then, spiritually speaking, we also died.

**Study 4. Why God Accepts Us. Galatians 3:1-14.**

*Purpose:* To realize that God accepts us not because of what *we* do but rather because of what *Christ* has done for us.

**Question 2.** This question should lead you to a broad understanding of what had happened to the Galatians between the time Paul first preached to them and the writing of this letter.

**Question 3.** There is a lot in these verses, so don't be satisfied with one or two answers. Paul asks five questions in verses 1-5, and each one points out something foolish in the Galatians' behavior.

This is the first time Paul mentions the Holy Spirit. He contrasts relying on the Spirit with relying on human effort (literally "the flesh"). This contrast is picked up again and expanded later on in the letter.

**Question 4.** You may skip this if the group gave a full answer to question 1.

**Question 6.** Paul stresses that faith is not a new concept—after all, Abraham believed. Likewise, faith does not conflict with God's original plans for Abraham, which envisioned worldwide blessing through faith in Christ.

Regarding verse 7, F. F. Bruce writes, "The Galatians were being urged [by the Judaizers] to become children of Abraham by adoption (since they were not his children by natural birth), and this, they were told, involved circumcision, just as it did for proselytes from paganism to Judaism. Paul maintains that, having believed the gospel and received God's gift of righteousness, they are Abraham's children already, in the only sense that matters in God's sight" (F. F. Bruce, *Galatians,* p. 155).

**Question 8.** Christ redeemed us in order that we might receive the "blessing given to Abraham" and "the promises of the Spirit" (v. 14). Are these two purposes or one? Many commentators believe that verse 14 speaks of only one purpose of Christ's redemption. The two phrases "in order that" and "so that" are parallel in Greek (see also RSV) and may be two ways of describing the same thing—the first description being general and the second specific. If this view is correct, then the gift of the Spirit *is* the promised blessing.

**Question 10.** This is an important question. Help the group to see that God accepts us so completely that he comes to live within us through the Spirit.

**Question 11.** After studying this passage, words such as *crucified, Spirit, righteousness* and *blessing* should bring to mind a number of reasons for thanking and praising God for what he has done for us in Christ.

**Study 5. Exposing Our Needs. Galatians 3:15-29.**

*Purpose:* To realize God gave the law not to save us but to expose our need for Christ.

**Question 2.** Make sure the group focuses on how a human covenant is similar to God's covenant with Abraham. In verse 16 Paul says "the promises were spoken to Abraham and to his seed." He probably has in mind several Old Testament passages, especially Genesis 22:18: "Through your offspring [sometimes translated "seed"] all nations on earth will be blessed." The word *seed* in Hebrew, Greek and English is a collective singular and can refer to a single descendant or to many descendants. Paul claims that *seed* ultimately referred to Christ.

In verse 17 Paul says that the law was introduced 430 years after God's covenant with Abraham. Exodus 12:40 states that "the length of time the Israelite people lived in Egypt was 430 years." This verse would indicate that the period from Abraham to the giving of the law was longer than 430 years. However, the Samaritan Pentateuch and the Septuagint, a popular Greek translation of the New Testament, read: "The length of time the Israelite people lived in Egypt *and in Canaan* was 430 years." Paul may have been quoting from the Septuagint. Yet whatever the explanation, the number of years is peripheral to his argument. Therefore, if the issue arises, suggest that it might be better to discuss this after the study is over so your attention can focus on the main points.

**Question 3.** One purpose of the law was to be "in charge" of us and to have "supervision" over us (vv. 24-25). This supervisor, known as a *pedagogue* in Greek and Roman society, was a slave who was put in charge of a minor until he reached adulthood. Such slaves were often pictured with a rod or cane in their hands. A modern analogy would be a strict governess. John Stott writes: "Like a gaoler [the law] has thrown us into prison; like a *paidagogos* it rebukes and punishes us for our misdeeds."

The group may wonder about the meaning of verse 20. It might interest you to know that more than three hundred different interpretations have been suggested for this verse! However, the Living Bible may have captured its meaning: "God gave his laws to angels to give to Moses, who then gave them to the people; but when God gave his promise to Abraham, he did it by himself alone, without angels or Moses as go-betweens" (vv. 19b-20). Paul's point is that the law is inferior to the promise because the former came indirectly and the latter directly.

**Question 6.** John Stott writes: "Not until the law has arrested and imprisoned us will we pine for Christ to set us free. Not until the law has condemned and killed us will we call upon Christ for justification and life. . . . Not until the law has humbled us even to hell will we turn to the gospel to raise us to heaven" (Stott, *Galatians,* p. 93).

**Question 8.** Galatians 3:28 has been wrongly interpreted as teaching that *all* racial, social and sexual distinctions have been abolished in Christ. Yet the Scriptures teach that there is God-given diversity within the body of Christ. We are all equal, but we are not all the same. The context clarifies what Paul means when he says we are all one in Christ (3:28).

**Study 6. The Joys of Growing Up. Galatians 4:1-20.**
*Purpose:* To realize some of our privileges as God's sons and daughters, especially when compared to the lives of those who were under the law.
**Question 3.** The group might notice that in verse 3 the Greek word *stoicheia* is translated "basic principles" by the NIV and "elemental spirits" by the RSV. At first glance there seems to be no logical connection between the two. But the relationship between them is actually quite simple.

The Greeks thought of the letters of the alphabet as the "elements" of words and sentences. They also thought of earth, water, air and fire as the elements of the material world, and they tended to deify these elements and worship them. Only the context can ultimately determine whether Paul intended the word *stoicheia* to be understood as *basic principles* (a reference to the law) or as *elemental spirits* (as used of Greek deities). In verses 8-9 he may have both meanings in mind. Obviously you don't need to mention this if there are no questions about it in the group.
**Question 4.** John Stott helps us answer the question, "Why is the period of Christ's coming termed 'the fulness of time' (AV)? Various factors combined to make it such. For instance, it was the time when Rome had conquered and subdued the known inhabited earth, when Roman roads had been built to facilitate travel and Roman legions had been stationed to guard them. It was also the time when the Greek language and culture had given a certain cohesion to society. At the same time, the old mythological gods of Greece and Rome were losing their hold on the common people, so that the hearts and minds of men everywhere were hungry for a religion that was real and satisfying. Further, it was the time when the law of Moses had done its work of preparing men for Christ, holding them under its tutelage and in its prison, so that they longed ardently for the freedom with which Christ could make them free" (Stott, *Galatians,* p. 105-6).
**Question 9.** Paul's feelings are most clearly seen in his use of the metaphor of childbirth. Encourage your group to focus on the attitudes and feelings conveyed by this imagery.
**Looking ahead to Study 7.** Some members of your group may not be familiar with the Old Testament account of Hagar and Sarah (Gen 15—18, 21)

which forms the basis for the next study. If this is so, you or some other member of your group should be prepared to *briefly* summarize the main aspects of the story. Of course the best preparation would be to have your group read these chapters before coming to the study. Suggest this at the end of study six.

**Study 7. Do-It-Yourself Religion. Galatians 4:21—5:1.**
*Purpose:* To consider how do-it-yourself religion differs from trust in the promises and power of God.

Before you ask question 2, you may want to summarize the story of Sarah and Hagar (Gen 15—18, 21) or ask the group to do so based on the reading you asked them to do at the end of the last study.

**Questions 2-3.** Question 2 asks the group to *observe* the differences between Abraham's two sons. Question 3 asks them to *interpret* the meaning of these differences. If the group gives a full answer to question 2, then skip question 3.

**Question 4.** The kind of "allegory" Paul has in mind is known as typology. Typology has been defined as "a way of setting forth the biblical history of salvation so that some of its earlier phases [such as Hagar and Sarah] are seen as anticipations of later phases [such as the Old and New Covenants]" (J. D. Douglas, et al., eds., "Typology," *New Bible Dictionary,* 2nd ed. [Wheaton, Ill.: Tyndale, 1982]).

**Question 5.** Verse 27 is a quote from Isaiah 54:1. There the woman "who has a husband" refers to the city of Jerusalem before the Babylonian exile. It corresponds to Hagar. The "barren woman" refers to Jerusalem after the Babylonians have carried off her children and left her desolate. It corresponds to Sarah. God promises that after the exile Jerusalem will be rebuilt and restored to a position of unsurpassed glory. But Paul sees the ultimate fulfillment of the prophecy in the New Jerusalem, the eternal dwelling place of the people of God.

**Question 6.** As your group discusses the differences between salvation by faith and salvation by observing the law, be sure they also discuss how they are *illustrated* by the two sons (especially), covenants and cities.

**Question 7.** Your group might want to consider persecution by religious as well as non-religious people. As John Stott writes about verse 29, "The persecution of the true church, of Christian believers who trace their spiritual descent from Abraham, is not always by the world, who are strangers unrelated to us, but by our half-brothers, religious people, the nominal church. It has always been so. The Lord Jesus was bitterly opposed, rejected, mocked and condemned by His own nation. The fiercest opponents of the apostle Paul, who dogged his footsteps and stirred up strife against him, were the official church, the Jews. . . . And the greatest enemies of the evangelical faith today are not unbelievers, who when they hear the gospel often embrace it, but the church, the establishment, the hierarchy. Isaac always mocked and persecuted by Ishmael" (Stott, *Galatians,* p. 127).

**Questions 10-11.** The fact that 5:1 begins a new chapter obscures the fact that it is naturally linked to 4:31. When the two verses are read together, this becomes clearer.

**Study 8. A Severe Warning. Galatians 5:2-12.**

*Purpose:* To understand the serious consequences of embracing a perverted gospel.

**Question 3.** Paul makes several disturbing statements. Chances are that someone in your group will feel personally or theologically threatened by what Paul is saying—especially with the warning "you have fallen away from grace."

It is natural for questions about the doctrine of eternal security to arise in peoples' minds when reading a passage such as this. But you might point out that Paul's major concern here is neither to confirm nor deny that doctrine. He is not raising the question, "Are Christians eternally secure?" but rather, "What are the consequences when a person embraces a perverted gospel?" Urge your group to seriously consider what Paul *is* saying rather than what he has left unsaid.

Nonetheless, what Paul is saying is so harsh that we are tempted to explain it away rather than truly explaining it. In the process a discussion of eternal security may be unavoidable. Therefore, consider the following.

Paul's statements should be allowed their full force. In the strongest possible language he states that if a person embraces a perverted gospel, he or she has no share in Christ or the grace that comes through him. In other words, no one can be saved by believing a false or perverted gospel.

But what about those who initially believe the true gospel, but later on embrace a perverted gospel? Do they *lose* their salvation? This question is framed in such a way as to make a satisfactory answer impossible. If the answer is no, Paul's words are emptied of their force. If the answer is yes, the scriptural emphasis on eternal security is denied. Yet both must somehow be maintained. Perhaps a better question might be, Would a true Christian embrace a false gospel? The answer is found in a doctrine known as the perseverance of the saints.

Eternal security looks at the Christian from God's perspective. But the corollary of eternal security—perseverance of the saints—looks at the Christian from the human perspective. The same Scriptures which teach eternal security also teach that a true Christian will persevere, by the power and grace of God, unto the end (1 Jn 2:19). There will be many struggles, failures and successes. But the fight will be fought, the race completed and the battle won. From God's point of view, the results are assured. Yet from our perspective, we need constant strength, encouragement and even warnings—such as the one in this passage—to keep us on course.

**Question 4.** The Galatians felt that they must believe in Christ *and* be circumcised in order to be saved.

**Question 8.** As in 1 Corinthians 5:6-7, yeast in verse 9 is compared to a negative influence that starts small but eventually affects the whole.

**Question 9.** "I am confident in the Lord that you will take no other view." Even though this is a brief statement, it is very significant in this context. Is this merely a tactful way of expressing wishful thinking? Is it based on Paul's knowledge of the Galatians and his confidence in them? How can he possibly believe that they will not give in to his opponents when the threat seems so serious? Wrestle with these issues!

### Study 9. Living by the Spirit. Galatians 5:13-26.

*Purpose:* To understand the true meaning of Christian freedom and how our lives can be transformed by the Spirit.

**Question 4.** The word *live* in verse 16 is a translation of the Greek word for *walk* (see NASB, RSV). It refers to our conduct, the manner in which we live.

The RSV translates the second half of verse 16 as a command: "and *do not* gratify the desire of the flesh" (my emphasis). The NIV translation ("you *will not*") is better. Paul strongly assures us that if we live by the Spirit we will not (and could not possibly) gratify the desires of the sinful nature.

**Question 5.** It is common to interpret verse 17 as though it were describing a frustrating conflict between the Spirit and our sinful nature which results in a spiritual deadlock.

The conflict is certainly real. If we seek to follow the desires of the sinful nature, the Spirit opposes us. Either way we face opposition! But if Paul is claiming that the conflict results in a spiritual deadlock, then he is contradicting rather than supporting the strong assurance he gave in verse 16. This means that it is essential for your group to keep from interpreting verse 17 in isolation. It was written to confirm and elaborate verse 16!

**Question 6.** The Spirit's leading in verse 18 has nothing to do with guidance. He is leading us toward moral and spiritual maturity.

**Question 8.** See comments on eternal security in leader's notes for study eight, question 3.

**Question 11.** The word for *live* in verse 25 is different from the word translated "live" in verse 16 (NIV). The word in verse 25 refers to the Spirit as the source of our *life*. In verse 16 the word literally means "walk" (see note to question 4) and refers to the Spirit as the one who enables us to live differently as Christians. It stresses *conduct*. It would seem that all three expressions—walking by the Spirit (v. 16), being led by the Spirit (v. 18) and living by the Spirit (v. 25)—are closely related facets of the Spirit's ministry in us.

### Study 10. The Law of Love. Galatians 6:1-10.

*Purpose:* To encourage us to build healthy and supportive relationships with other Christians and non-Christians.

**Question 1.** This question is designed to help your group to observe the basic structure of this passage and to give them a *brief* overview of what Paul is discussing.

**Question 2.** The first part of question 2 should give the members of your group a greater appreciation for Paul's guidelines for dealing with a person caught in a sin.

John Stott tells us that the Greek word translated "restore" (v. 1) "was used in secular Greek as a medical term for setting a fractured or dislocated bone. It is applied in Mark 1:19 to the apostles who were 'mending' their nets, although Arndt-Gingrich suggest a wider interpretation, namely that after a night's fishing, they were 'overhauling' (NEB) their nets 'by cleaning, mending, folding (them) together' " (Stott, *Galatians,* p. 160).

**Question 5.** Someone in your group may wonder whether Paul's statement "each one should carry his own load" (v. 5) contradicts his command to "carry each other's burdens" (v. 2). Rather than giving your own answer to this question, ask that person (or the group) how he or she thinks the two statements can be reconciled. If they have difficulty answering this question, you might point out that there is a difference between the words "carry each other's *burdens*" and "carry his own *load*." The former has in mind any oppressive difficulty which a person is facing. The latter stresses that we are each responsible to God for our own attitudes and actions.

**Question 7.** The principle "a man reaps what he sows" is very broad and has a number of applications. For example, Paul immediately applies it to sowing the sinful nature or the Spirit (v. 8). He also alludes to it when he talks about "doing good" (v. 9). But his discussion of the principle was probably prompted by the thought of Christians hoarding their money or squandering it rather than using it to help others—in this case those who teach them the Scriptures (see v. 6).

It is possible for verse 8 to be interpreted in such a way that it contradicts Paul's emphasis on justification by faith. Therefore, it might be helpful to ask your group how the two can be harmonized.

**Question 9.** It isn't necessary for everyone in the group to share how they intend to apply this principle. But even those who don't share should be encouraged to silently commit their plans to God during the time of prayer.

### Study 11. Getting Motivated. Galatians 6:11-18.

*Purpose:* To reflect on our primary motives and goals in life.

**Verse 11.** Various other suggestions have been made concerning the "large letters" of verse 11. Some commentators believe that Paul had bad eyesight and refer to Galatians 4:13-15 for support. Others believe that his writing was large (and sloppy?) because he was not a professional scribe. However, given the urgent nature of his letter, the idea of emphasis seems most plausible.

**Questions 5-6.** If the group has difficulty answering these questions, ask, "How does Paul's attitude toward boasting differ from the world's attitude?" People in "the world" (non-Christian society) boast in their own accomplishments in order to gain the respect and admiration of others. Paul has put to death ("crucified") this kind of attitude. He boasts in Christ not himself. He seeks Christ's approval not the world's. Because of Paul's attitudes the world persecutes him and would crucify him if they could.

**Questions 9-10.** "The Greek word for 'marks' is *stigmata.* Medieval churchmen believed that these were the scars in the hands, feet and side of Jesus, and that Paul by sympathetic identification with Him found the same scars appearing in his body. . . . It is most unlikely, however, that the *stigmata* of Jesus which Paul bore on his body were of this kind. Doubtless they were rather wounds which he had received while being persecuted for Jesus' sake" (Stott, *Galatians,* pp. 181-82). These wounds proved that he was Christ's servant. Paul did not hesitate to preach the cross of Christ, or to do anything for Christ's sake, even if it meant persecution.

### Study 12. Galatians Today. Galatians 1—6.

*Purpose:* To review the major ideas presented in Galatians and to grapple with how the principles you've learned in Galatians apply to problems we face today.

**Question 1.** There are a myriad of ideas discussed in Galatians but only a few major themes. Concentrate on these. Try to avoid a lengthy discussion, however, since most of these ideas are touched on elsewhere in this study.

**Question 3.** For example, any idea of human merit must be excluded from a proper presentation of the gospel and personal boasting must be excluded from any proper response.

**Question 4.** This statement comes from Robert H. Schuller's book *Self-Esteem: The New Reformation* (Waco, Tex.: Word Books, 1982), p. 39. The question is designed to call to mind and apply Paul's statements about his God-given authority and the source of his message (Gal 1—2).

**Question 5.** You may be surprised to find that some members of your group will believe that this is a perverted statement of the gospel while others will not. If necessary, ask them to consider how this statement of the gospel differs from that of Paul's opponents. They would probably have affirmed the following:

a. I must believe in Jesus Christ and thereby receive the forgiveness he offers through his death on the cross.

b. I must be circumcised.

c. I must seek to obey the law of God (with the help of the Spirit of God). Are points b and c different, in principle, from b and c in question 5?

**Question 6.** This question could result in a heated discussion. It is important that the members of your group truly listen to each other, and that they respect each other's differences.

**Question 7.** Remember, the question is not whether the members of your group are personally for or against such practices. It concerns whether rules such as these, as critics claim, place too little confidence in the Spirit's ability to regulate a Christian's behavior.

*Jack Kubatschek, a former staff member with InterVarsity Christian Fellowship, is Bible study editor for InterVarsity Press. He is the author of* How to Study the Bible *and the LifeGuide Bible Study* Romans *and coauthor (with James Nyquist) of* Leading Bible Discussions: Revised Edition *(all from IVP).*